piano · vocal · guitar

contents

ISBN 978-1-4584-0545-6

HAL·LEONARD®
CORPORATION

7777 W. BLUEMOUND RD. P.O. BOX 13819 MILWAUKEE, WI 53213

Visit Hal Leonard Online at
www.halleonard.com

BAD BOYS

Words and Music by
IAN MUNTY LEWIS

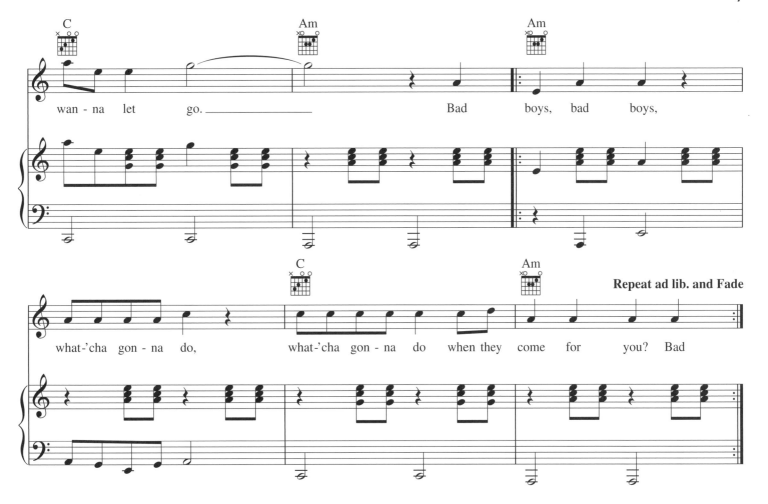

wan - na let go. _____ Bad boys, bad boys,

Repeat ad lib. and Fade

what-'cha gon - na do, what-'cha gon - na do when they come for you? Bad

Additional Lyrics

2. You chuck it on that one,
   You chuck it on this one,
   You chuck it on your mother
   And you chuck it on your father.
   You chuck it on your brother
   And you chuck it on your sister,
   You chuck it on that one
   And you chuck it on me.
   Chorus

3. Nobody naw give you no breaks,
   Police naw give you no breaks,
   Soldier naw give you no breaks,
   Not even your idren naw give you no breaks.
   Chorus

CHERRY OH BABY

Words and Music by
ERIC DONALDSON

1865
(96 Degress in the Shade)

Words and Music by WILLIAM CLARK,
MICHAEL COOPER and STEPHEN COORE

Slow Reggae groove

Nine-ty-six de-grees in the shade. Real hot in the

shade. Said it was nine-ty-six de-grees in the

shade, ten thou-sand sol-diers on pa-

EQUAL RIGHTS

Words and Music by
PETER TOSH

Moderate Reggae

V103 DV106
S45 (J76)

Ev-'ry-one is cry-ing out __ for peace, yes. None is cry-ing out for

54 46, THAT'S MY NUMBER

Words and Music by
FREDERICK HIBBERT

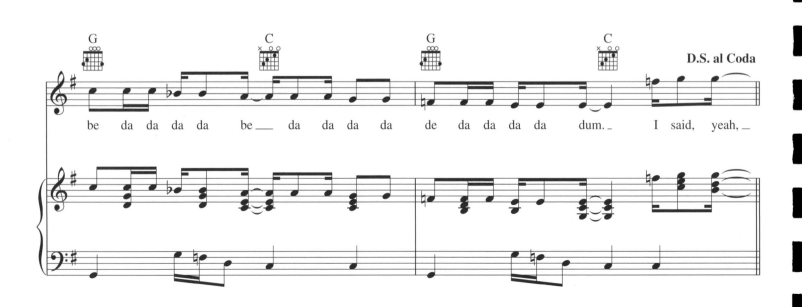

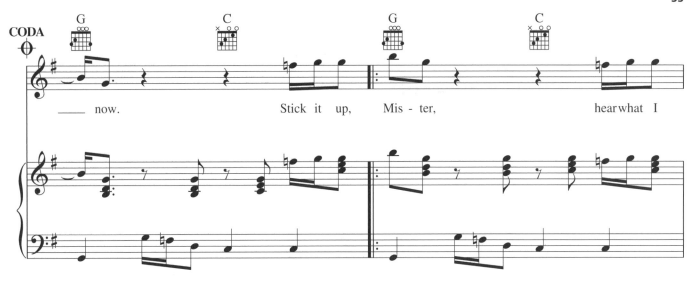

now. Stick it up, Mis - ter, hearwhat I

say, sir. Get your hands in the air, sir, and you will get no hurt, __

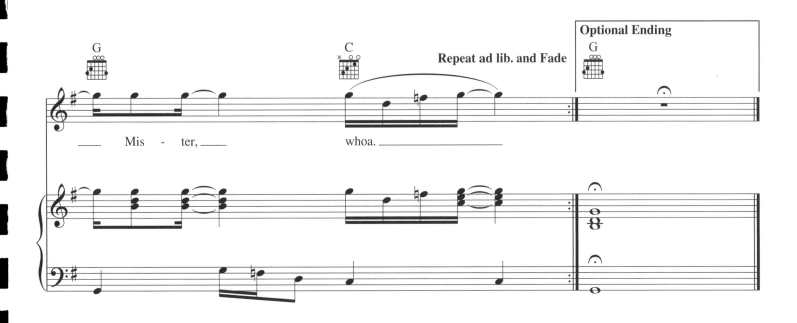

__ Mis - ter, __ whoa. __

FUNKY KINGSTON

V103 DV 194/195

S166(T99)

Words and Music by
FREDERICK HIBBERT

Moderate Reggae feel

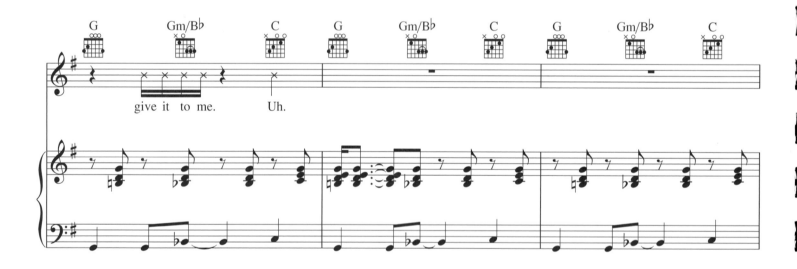

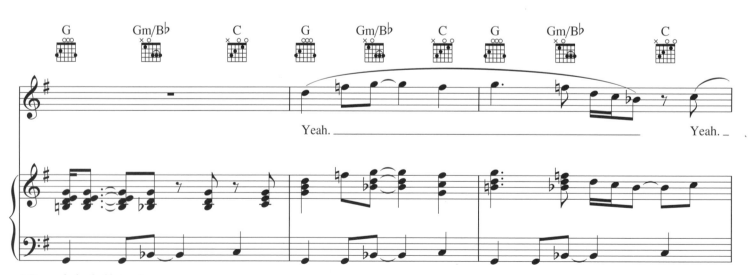

* Recorded a half step lower.

GET UP STAND UP

Words and Music by BOB MARLEY
and PETER TOSH

Get up, stand up, don't give up ___ the fight.
Get up, stand up, don't give up ___ the fight.
Get up, stand up, don't give up ___ the fight. We're

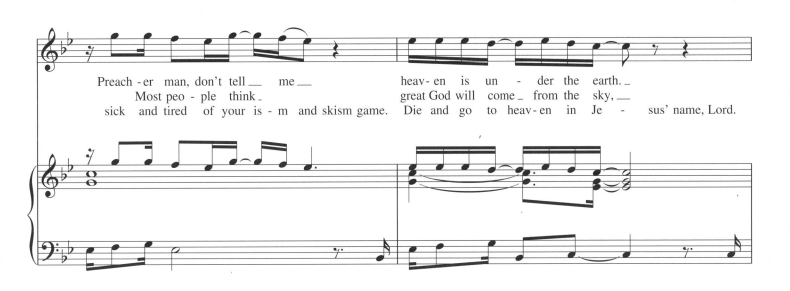

Preach - er man, don't tell ___ me ___ heav - en is un - der the earth. ___
Most peo - ple think ___ great God will come ___ from the sky, ___
sick and tired of your is - m and skism game. Die and go to heav - en in Je - sus' name, Lord.

I know you don't ___ know what ___ life is real - ly worth. ___ Is not all ___
take a - way ev - 'ry - thing, and make ev - 'ry - bod - y feel high. But
We know when we un - der - stand. Al - might - y God is a liv - ing man. ___ You can fool ___

I SHOT THE SHERIFF

Words and Music by
BOB MARLEY

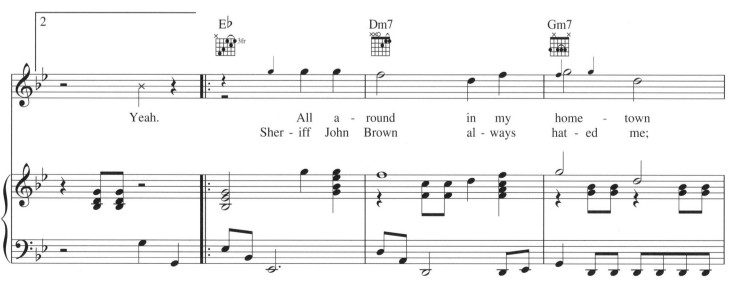

GUESS WHO'S COMING TO DINNER

Words and Music by
MICHAEL ROSE

Recorded a half step lower.

THE HARDER THEY COME

Words and Music by
JIMMY CLIFF

wait - ing for me when I die.
tryin' to drive me un - der - ground.
though I know that when you're dead you can't.

But be - tween the day you're born and a - when you die,
And they think that they have got the bat - tle won.
But I'd rath - er be a free man in my grave,

they nev - er seem to hear
I say for - give them, Lord, they know
than liv - ing as a pup -

e - ven your cry.
not what they've done.
- pet or a slave.

So as
'Cause as
So as

sure as the sun will shine,

I'm gon - na get my share now, what's mine.

And then the hard - er they come,

I CAN SEE CLEARLY NOW

Words and Music by
JOHNNY NASH

THE ISRAELITES

Words and Music by
DESMOND DEKKER

S69 (T146)

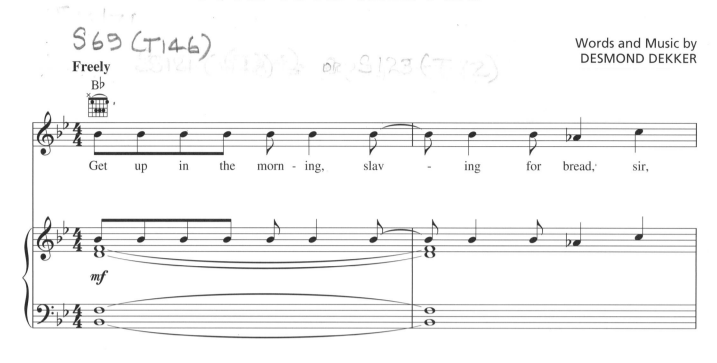

Get up in the morn-ing, slav-ing for bread, sir,

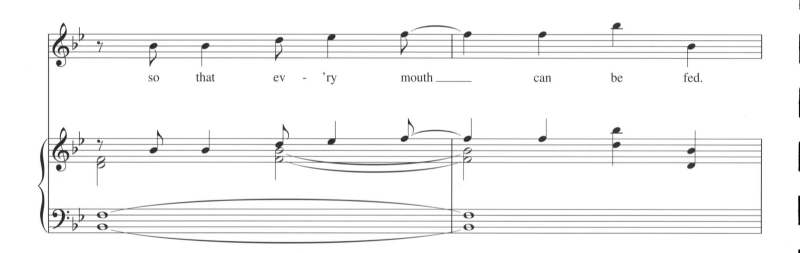

so that ev-'ry mouth ____ can be fed.

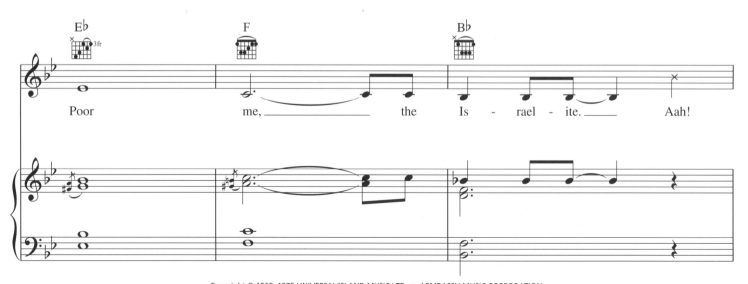

Poor me, ____ the Is-rael-ite. ____ Aah!

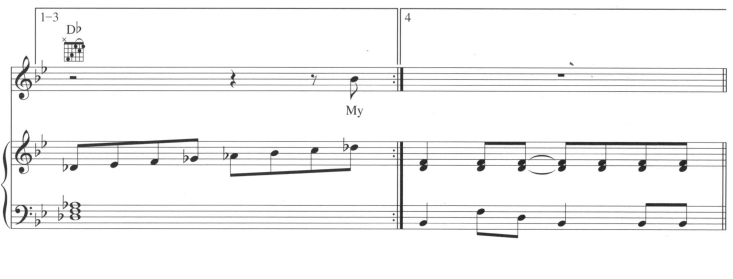

Additional Lyrics

2. My wife and my kids, they pack up and leave me;
   "Darling," she said, "I'm yours to receive."
   Poor me, the Israelite. Aah!

3. Shirt them ah tear up, trousers are gone;
   I don't want to end up like Bonnie and Clyde.
   Poor me, the Israelite. Aah!

4. After a storm there must be a calm,
   They catch me in the farm, you sound the alarm.
   Poor me, the Israelite. Aah!

JOHNNY TOO BAD

Words and Music by WINSTON BAILEY,
HYLTON BECKFORD, DERRICK CROOKS
and TREVOR WILSON

Slow Reggae groove

S91 (T82)
S66 (T99)   UB40

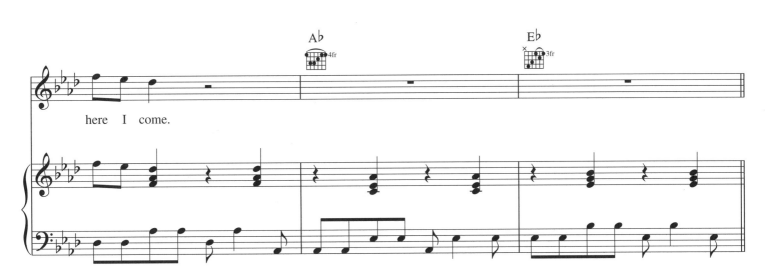

LEGALIZE IT

Words and Music by
PETER TOSH

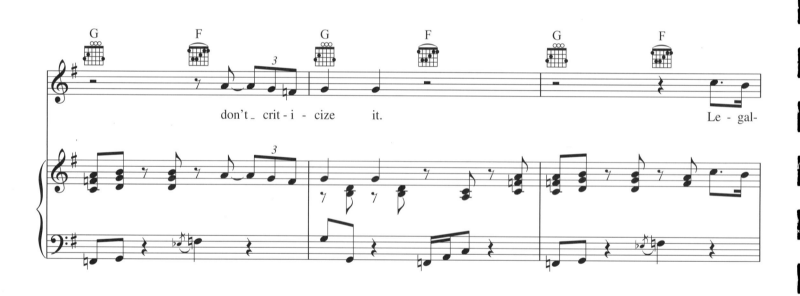

MANY RIVERS TO CROSS

Words and Music by
JIMMY CLIFF

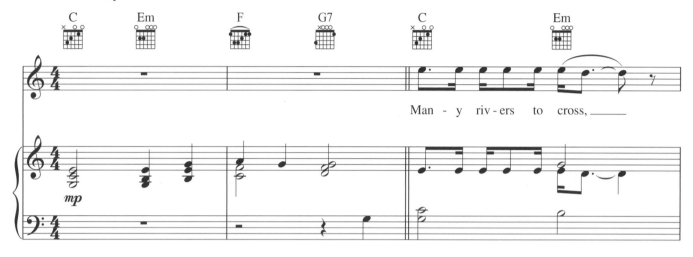

Moderately slow

Man - y riv - ers to cross, _____

but I can't seem to find my __ way _ o - ver.

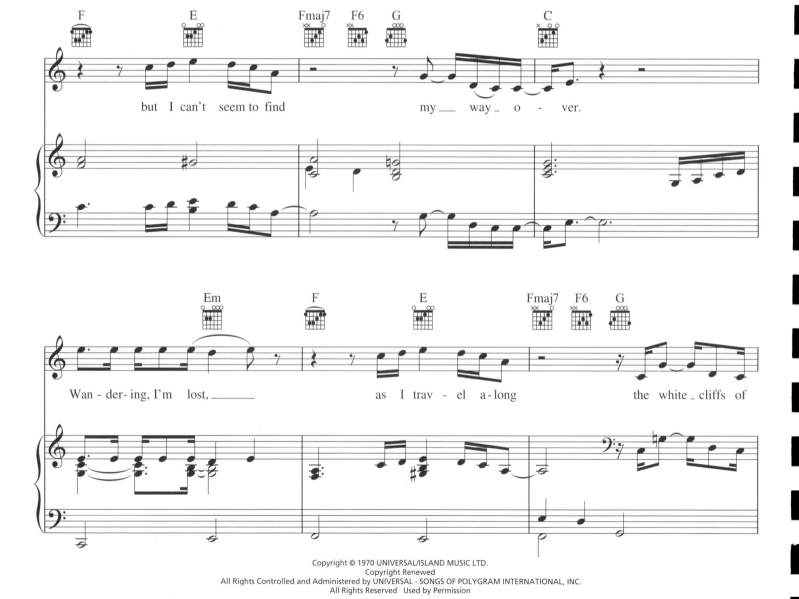

Wan - der - ing, I'm lost, _____ as I trav - el a - long the white _ cliffs of

MARCUS GARVEY

Words and Music by PHILLIP FULLWOOD
and WINSTON RODNEY

A MESSAGE TO YOU RUDY

Words and Music by
ROBERT THOMPSON

Copyright © 1979 by Carlin Music Corp.
All Rights for the U.S. and Canada Controlled by Carbert Music Inc.
International Copyright Secured   All Rights Reserved
Used by Permission

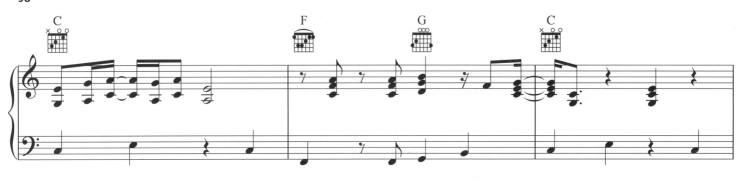

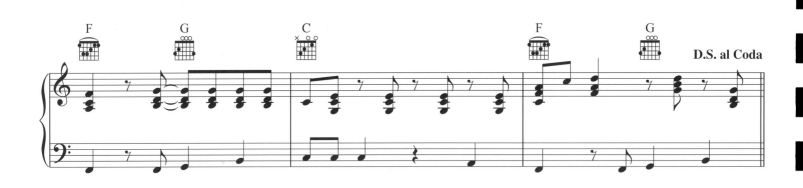

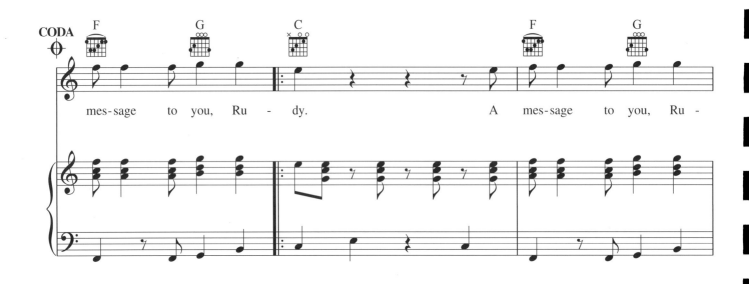

mes-sage to you, Ru - dy. A mes-sage to you, Ru -

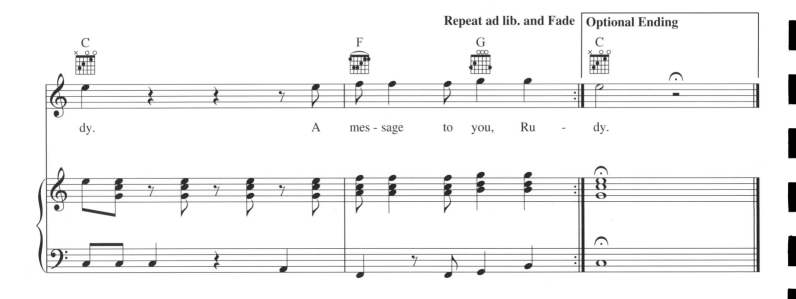

dy. A mes-sage to you, Ru - dy.

MONKEY MAN

Words and Music by
FREDERICK HIBBERT

With energy S63 (T128)

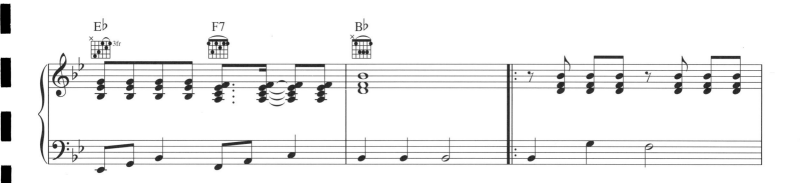

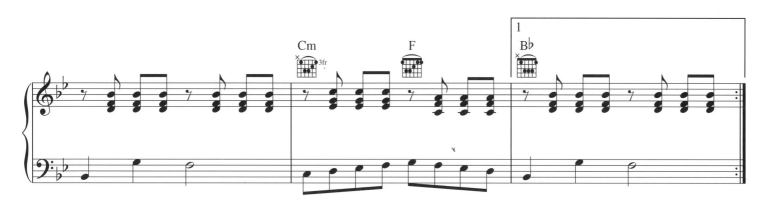

MURDER SHE WROTE

Words and Music by SLY DUNBAR,
LLOYD WILLIS, EVERTON BONNER
and JOHN TAYLOR

Rap Lyrics

I'll kill all of them.
A pretty fearsome bunchy come around town.
Then they kind of live in town,
All chopped up. Follow me.
A pretty fearsome bunch come around town.
Then they kind of live in town,
All discussin' that you're pretty,
They-a said, pretty bunch of character.
Dirty that you is-a up to.
Flirty, flirty, you are the town pick.
And are so-orry a-when you find your mischief.
You tell them you're sorry, sorry, sorry.

ONE LOVE

Strum Pattern 1
Relaxed Reggae beat

Words and Music by
BOB MARLEY

One love, ___ one heart. ___

Let's get to-geth-er and feel all right. { As it was in the be-
I'm plead-ing to ___ }

cry - ing. (One love.) ___ Hear the chil-dren cry - ing. (One heart.) ___ Say - in',
gin - ning, (One love.) ___ so shall it be in the end. ___ (One heart.) ___ Al - right, } "Give
man - kind. (One love.) ___ Oh, Lord. ___ (One heart.) ___ Whoa. ___

To Coda ⊕

NO WOMAN NO CRY

Words and Music by
VINCENT FORD

PARTY NEXT DOOR

Words and Music by
MICHAEL ROSE

PASS THE DUTCHIE

**Words and Music by DONAT ROY JACKIE MOTTO,
LLOYD FERGUSON, LEROY SIBBLES,
ROBERT LYN, HUFORD BROWN,
HEADLEY GEORGE BENNETT and FITZROY SIMPSON**

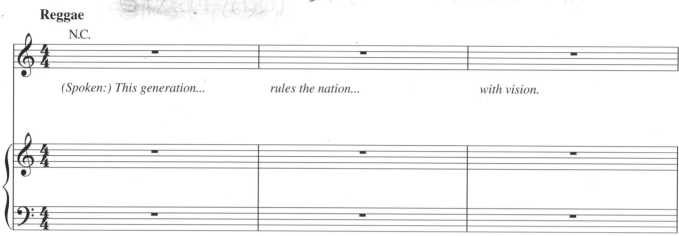

Reggae

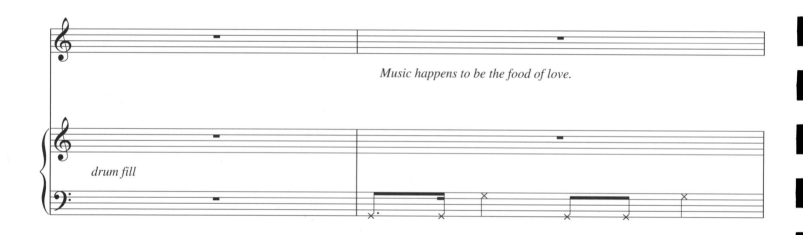

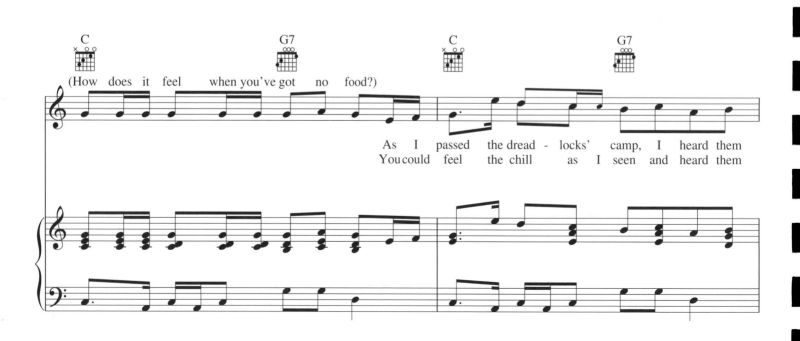

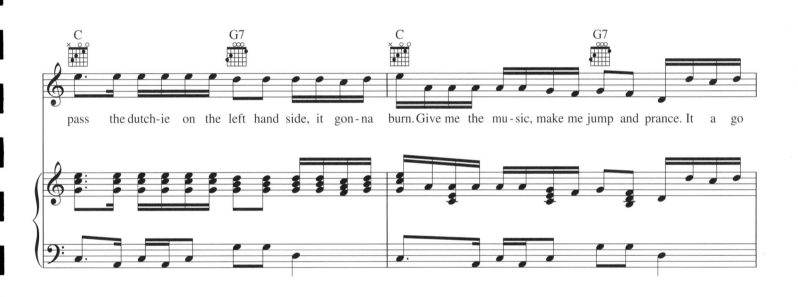

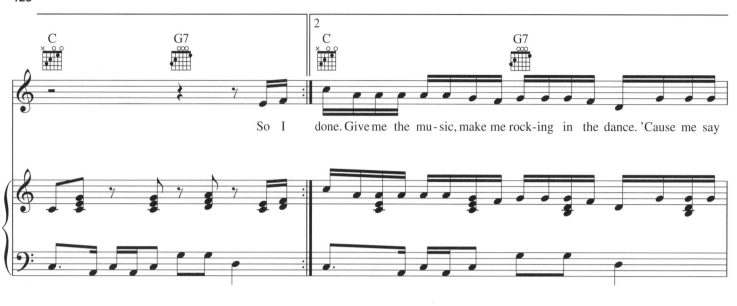

RED, RED WINE

Words and Music by
NEIL DIAMOND

V103 DV106

Moderately S160 (T88) VB40

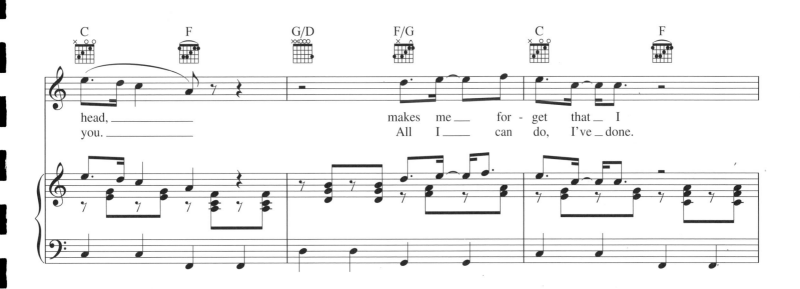

* Recorded a half step higher

POLICE AND THIEVES

Words and Music by JUNIOR MURVIN
and LEE PERRY

TURN BACK
2 PAGES

PRESSURE DROP

Words and Music by
FREDERICK HIBBERT

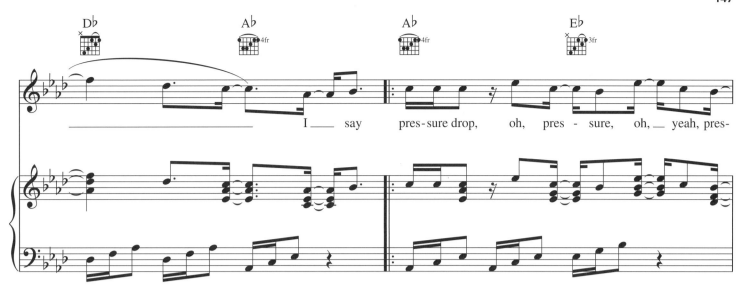

I ___ say pres-sure drop, oh, pres-sure, oh, ___ yeah, pres-

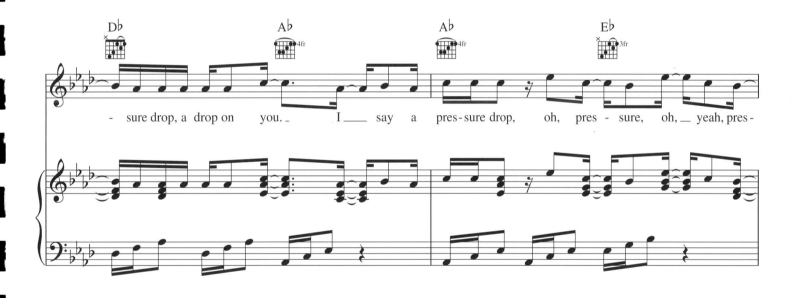

- sure drop, a drop on you. ___ I ___ say a pres-sure drop, oh, pres-sure, oh, ___ yeah, pres-

Repeat and Fade   **Optional Ending**

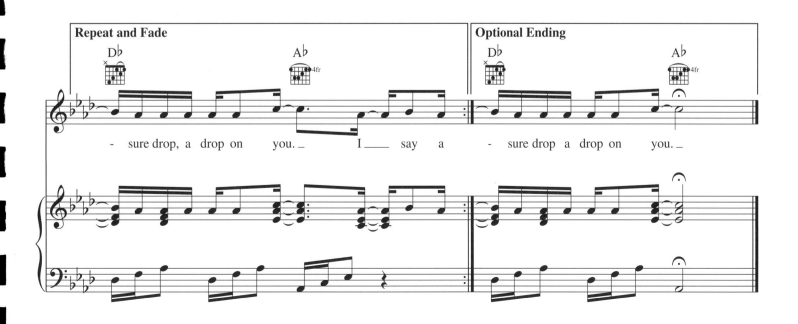

- sure drop, a drop on you. ___ I ___ say a   - sure drop a drop on you. ___

REDEMPTION SONG

Words and Music by
BOB MARLEY

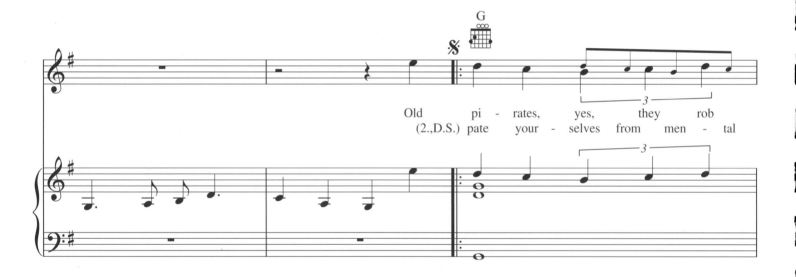

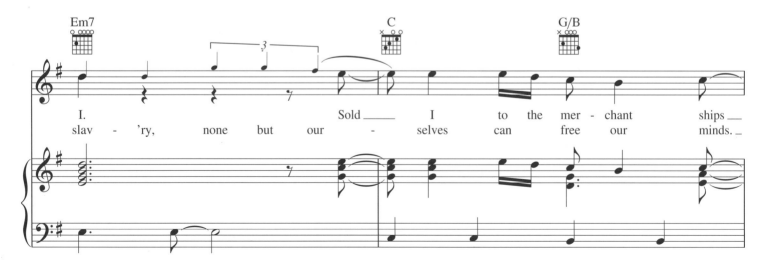

SITTING IN LIMBO

Words and Music by PLUMMER BRIGHTS
and JAMES CHAMBERS

Moderately, with movement

Sit - ting here — in lim - bo, but I know — it won't — be long. _____

Sit - ting here — in lim - bo, like a bird — with - out — a song. _

Well, they're

Sit-ting in lim - bo, sit-ting in

lim - bo._____ Sit-ting in lim - bo, sit-ting in

lim - bo._____

Sit - ting in

RIVERS OF BABYLON

Words and Music by BRENT DOWE,
JAMES A. McNAUGHTON, GEORGE REYAM
and FRANK FARIAN

Optional Ending

D.S. and Fade

SATTA-AMASAS-GANA

Words and Music by NEVILLE COLLINS,
DONALD MANNING and LINFORD MANNING

007 (SHANTY TOWN)

By DESMOND DEKKER

STIR IT UP

Words and Music by
BOB MARLEY

SWEET AND DANDY

Words and Music by
FREDERICK "TOOTS" HIBBERT

S92 (T158) Toots + Maytals

Moderate Reggae feel, with movement

(1.,4.) Yeah. ___ Et - ty in the room a cry, ___
(2.,5.) John - son in the room a fret, ___
(3.,6.) one pound ten for the wed - ding cake,

Repeat verse 1-3 on times 4-6

Ma - ma says she must wipe her eye. ___ Pa - pa says she no fi
Un - cle says he must hold up him head. Aunt - y says she no fi
plen - ty bot - tle of co - la wine. ___ All the peo - ple, them dress

fool - ish, like ___ she nev - er been to school ___ at all. ___
fool - ish like ___ a no time fi him wed - ding day. ___ It is no
up in a ___ white, fi go eat out John - son's wed - ding cake.

THREE LITTLE BIRDS

S 234 (T74)

Words and Music by
BOB MARLEY

Moderately slow Reggae

VIETNAM

Words and Music by
JIMMY CLIFF

With energy

Recorded a half step higher.

THE TIDE IS HIGH

Words and Music by JOHN HOLT,
TYRONE EVANS and HOWARD BARRETT

The tide is high, but I'm hold-ing on. I'm gon-na be your num-ber one. I'm _____ not the kind of man _____ who _____ gives up just _____ like that, _____ no. _____ It's

TOMORROW PEOPLE

Words and Music by
ZIGGY MARLEY

WANNA BE LOVED

Words and Music by WAYNE BROWNE,
DAVE KELLY, HOPETON LINDO
and MARK MYRIE

TURN 2 PAGES

Back 1 page to Coda

YOU CAN GET IT IF YOU REALLY WANT

Words and Music by
JIMMY CLIFF

With energy S204 (T128)

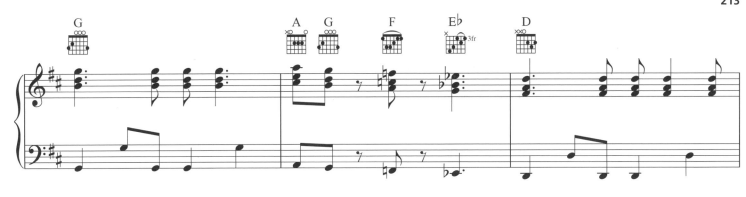

D.S. al Coda

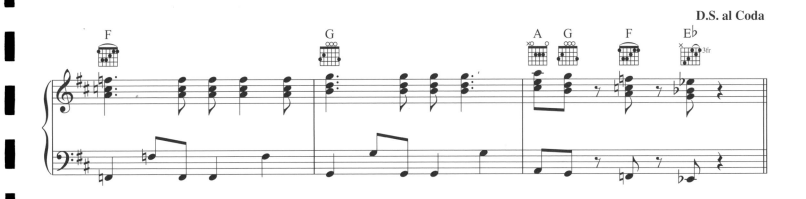

you'll suc-ceed at last.____ You can get it if you real-ly want.__

Lead vocal ad lib.

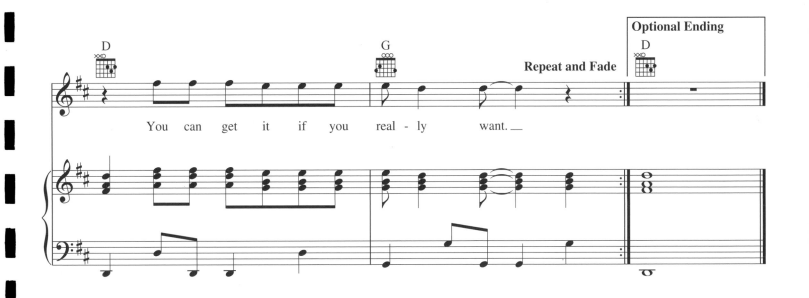

You can get it if you real-ly want.__

Repeat and Fade

Optional Ending

WESTBOUND TRAIN

Words and Music by WINSTON BOSWELL
and DENNIS BROWN

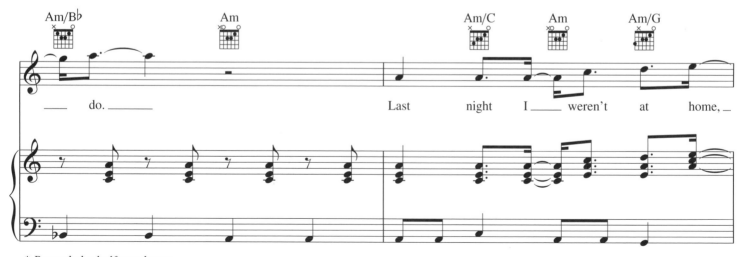

Recorded a half step lower.

WONDERFUL WORLD, BEAUTIFUL PEOPLE

Words and Music by
JIMMY CLIFF

With energy $155 (T106)

Hey, _____ yeah. Won-der-ful world, _____ beau-ti-ful peo-ple.

You are your girl _____ things could be pret-ty. But un-der-neath_ this

there is a se-cret that no-bod-y _____ can re-peat. _

THE ULTIMATE SERIES

This comprehensive series features jumbo collections of piano/vocal arrangements with guitar chords. Each volume features an outstanding selection of your favorite songs. Collect them all for the ultimate music library!

Blues
90 blues classics, including: Boom Boom • Born Under a Bad Sign • Gee Baby, Ain't I Good to You • I Can't Quit You Baby • Pride and Joy • (They Call It) Stormy Monday • Sweet Home Chicago • Why I Sing the Blues • and more.
00310723............................$19.95

Broadway Gold
100 show tunes: Beauty and the Beast • Do-Re-Mi • I Whistle a Happy Tune • The Lady Is a Tramp • Memory • My Funny Valentine • Oklahoma • Some Enchanted Evening • Summer Nights • Tomorrow • many more.
00361396............................$21.95

Broadway Platinum – Third Edition
100 popular Broadway show tunes, featuring: Consider Yourself • Getting to Know You • Gigi • Do You Hear the People Sing • I'll Be Seeing You • My Favorite Things • People • She Loves Me • Try to Remember • Younger Than Springtime • many more.
00311496............................$22.95

Children's Songbook – Second Edition
66 fun songs for kids: Alphabet Song • Be Our Guest • Bingo • The Brady Bunch • Do-Re-Mi • Hakuna Matata • It's a Small World • Kum Ba Yah • Sesame Street Theme • Tomorrow • Won't You Be My Neighbor? • and more.
00310690............................$19.99

Christmas – Third Edition
Includes: Carol of the Bells • Deck the Hall • Frosty the Snow Man • Gesu Bambino • Good King Wenceslas • Jingle-Bell Rock • Joy to the World • Nuttin' for Christmas • O Holy Night • Rudolph the Red-Nosed Reindeer • Silent Night • What Child Is This? • and more.
00361399............................$19.95

Classic Rock
70 rock classics in one great collection! Includes: Angie • Best of My Love • California Girls • Crazy Little Thing Called Love • Joy to the World • Landslide • Light My Fire • Livin' on a Prayer • (She's) Some Kind of Wonderful • Sultans of Swing • Sweet Emotion • and more.
00310962............................$22.95

Classical Collection
Delightful piano solo arrangements, including: Air on the G String (Bach) • Für Elise (Beethoven) • Seguidilla from Carmen (Bizet) • Lullaby (Brahms) • Clair De Lune (Debussy) • The Swan (Saint-Saëns) • Ave Maria (Schubert) • Swan Lake (Tchaikovsky) • dozens more.
00311109............................$17.95

Contemporary Christian
Includes over 40 favorites: Awesome God • Can't Live a Day • El Shaddai • Friends • God Is in Control • His Strength Is Perfect • I Can Only Imagine • One of These Days • Place in This World • and more.
00311224............................$19.95

Country – Second Edition
90 of your favorite country hits: Boot Scootin' Boogie • Chattahoochie • Could I Have This Dance • Crazy • Down at the Twist And Shout • Hey, Good Lookin' • Lucille • When She Cries • and more.
00310036............................$19.95

Gospel
Includes: El Shaddai • His Eye Is on the Sparrow • How Great Thou Art • Just a Closer Walk With Thee • Lead Me, Guide Me • (There'll Be) Peace in the Valley (For Me) • Precious Lord, Take My Hand • Wings of a Dove • and more.
00241009............................$19.95

Jazz Standards
Over 100 great jazz favorites: Ain't Misbehavin' • All of Me • Come Rain or Come Shine • Here's That Rainy Day • I'll Take Romance • Imagination • Li'l Darlin' • Manhattan • Moonglow • Moonlight in Vermont • A Night in Tunisia • The Party's Over • Solitude • Star Dust • and more.
00361407............................$19.95

Latin Songs
80 hot Latin favorites, including: Amapola (Pretty Little Poppy) • Amor • Bésame Mucho (Kiss Me Much) • Blame It on the Bossa Nova • Feelings (¿Dime?) • Malagueña • Mambo No. 5 • Perfidia • Slightly out of Tune (Desafinado) • What a Diff'rence a Day Made • and more.
00310689............................$19.99

Love and Wedding Songbook
90 songs of devotion including: The Anniversary Waltz • Canon in D • Endless Love • Forever and Ever, Amen • Just the Way You Are • Love Me Tender • Sunrise, Sunset • Through the Years • Trumpet Voluntary • and more.
00361445............................$19.95

Movie Music – Second Edition
73 favorites from the big screen, including: Can You Feel the Love Tonight • Chariots of Fire • Cruella De Vil • Driving Miss Daisy • Easter Parade • Forrest Gump • Moon River • That Thing You Do! • Viva Las Vegas • The Way We Were • When I Fall in Love • and more.
00310240............................$18.95

New Age
Includes: Cast Your Fate to the Wind • Chariots of Fire • Cristofori's Dream • A Day Without Rain • The Memory of Trees • The Steamroller • and more.
00311160............................$17.95

Reggae
42 favorite reggae hits, including: Get Up Stand Up • I Need a Roof • Jamaica Nice • Legalize It • Miss Jamaica • Rivers of Babylon • Tomorrow People • Uptown Top Ranking • Train to Skaville • Try Jah Love • and more.
00311029............................$18.95

Rock 'N' Roll
100 classics, including: All Shook Up • Bye Bye Love • Duke of Earl • Gloria • Hello Mary Lou • It's My Party • Johnny B. Goode • The Loco-Motion • Lollipop • Surfin' U.S.A. • The Twist • Wooly Bully • Yakety Yak • and more.
00361411............................$21.95

Singalong!
100 of the best-loved popular songs ever: Beer Barrel Polka • Crying in the Chapel • Edelweiss • Feelings • Five Foot Two, Eyes of Blue • For Me and My Gal • Indiana • It's a Small World • Que Sera, Sera • This Land Is Your Land • When Irish Eyes Are Smiling • and more.
00361418............................$18.95

Standard Ballads – Second Edition
91 mellow masterpieces, including: Angel Eyes • Body and Soul • Darn That Dream • Day By Day • Easy to Love • Mona Lisa • Moon River • My Funny Valentine • Smoke Gets in Your Eyes • When I Fall in Love • and more.
00310246............................$19.95

Swing Standards
93 songs to get you swinging, including: Bandstand Boogie • Boogie Woogie Bugle Boy • Heart and Soul • How High the Moon • In the Mood • Moonglow • Satin Doll • Sentimental Journey • Witchcraft • and more.
00310245............................$19.95

TV Themes
More than 90 themes from your favorite TV shows, including: The Addams Family Theme • Cleveland Rocks • Theme from Frasier • Happy Days • Love Boat Theme • Hey, Hey We're the Monkees • Nadia's Theme • Sesame Street Theme • Theme from Star Trek® • and more.
00310841............................$19.95

Prices, contents, and availability subject to change without notice.
Availability and pricing may vary outside the U.S.A.

FOR MORE INFORMATION, SEE YOUR LOCAL MUSIC DEALER, OR WRITE TO:

HAL•LEONARD®
CORPORATION
7777 W. BLUEMOUND RD. P.O. BOX 13819 MILWAUKEE, WI 53213

www.halleonard.com

1012